You are Not

Who You Think You Are

Poems that can awaken you

Sarfraz Zaidi, MD

You Are Not Who You Think You Are
Poems that can awaken you

First Edition, 2015

ISBN-13: 978-1500689032
ISBN-10: 1500689033

iComet Press

6988 Calle Dia, Camarillo, CA 93012

http://www.icometpress.com

Printed in the United States of America.

Disclaimer

The information contained in this book is general and is offered with no guarantees on the part of the author or publisher. The author and publisher disclaim all liability in connection with the use of this book. Any duplication or distribution of information contained herein is strictly prohibited.

Contents

Introduction

I am Sarfraz Zaidi, a medical doctor specializing in Diabetes and Endocrinology. As an endocrinologist, I became fully aware of the complexities of the human brain, and how stress can disrupt the normal functioning of the entire hormonal system in the body. But, what really is stress? How does it affect your body, and is it possible to manage stress without medications? For years, I was intrigued by these questions.

Then, one day, as I was walking in our neighborhood park pondering over these questions, I suddenly got the answers. A profound wisdom sank in. Things became crystal clear. You could call it enlightenment!

With this awakening, I felt a huge psychological load lift off my shoulders. I experienced a true psychological freedom. Now I feel a sense of joy and peace inside me which is hard to describe in words.

My outlook on life has completely changed. Now, I fully experience every moment of life. *I truly live in the now*. I am joyful and peaceful all the time. I stay completely free of stress, even under quite stressful situations. I call it the *ultimate freedom*. For example, a few years ago, I encountered a serious medical illness, which drained all energy out of me; I lost a lot of weight and looked like someone from the concentration camp, as my wife bluntly told me one day. During this time, I was admitted to the hospital twice, but doctors still could not accurately figure out my medical condition. The "old me" would have been very anxious, disappointed and depressed over this whole dreadful situation. Fortunately, this illness happened after my enlightenment. I walked on this frightening road with such a peace that even I was amazed at myself! Not for a moment was I depressed, disappointed, angry or anxious. Slowly, this medical situation resolved, without any medications. I believe my inner peace and energy provided immense healing power from within.

In my personal life, my wife, daughter and friends find me calmer, happier and joyful. Now I go to my office to make a reasonable living and help my patients. My memory is sharper than ever. *I don't even forget where I put my car keys anymore.* Whatever activity I am involved in, I do it better than I did before, but always with a sense of calmness and peace.

I don't create stress for myself or for anyone else! Actually people around me feel peaceful as well. Now I have realized that true peace has a ripple effect and it starts from you.

Every now and then, I feel like expressing wisdom through poems. Then, I sit down and let out whatever wants to come out. During these periods, I am utterly in the Now. Over the years, these poems have piled up. It is time to let them out, so others can benefit from them.

In this book, I share with you my earnest and sincere observations about life. You may agree or disagree and that's fine! I'm not trying to convince you. In no way, I am trying to upset anyone's feelings. *What I describe are my observations based upon logic.* I am not judging or criticizing anyone, or any group of people. I do not have any affiliation with any political party or religious organization. You may or may not agree with me, but please think; and think logically with an open-mind. After all, it is your life. I am simply inviting you to take a fresh look at it with logic.

First Of All

First of all,
let me explain
some simple facts
about these poems that I write,
without going to a poetry school.

I write them only when they flow in,
like the flow of the ocean breeze.

I do not subject these poems
to the torture of a grammar school,
to keep them fresh and original,
like a newborn child
without any stains
from her mother, father or a teacher

In case, you find yourself
irritated, annoyed and anxious
to correct all those grammar errors
to bring these poems
within the rigid confines of the form,
we conventionally call poems.

I suggest that you hang on
until you get to the end.
By then, you may change your mind.
In case, that you don't
I offer you my sincere apology.

New Year Day or Is It?

Happy New Year, I greeted the dog.
But, there was no reply.
Happy New Year, I greeted the cat.
But, there was no reply.
Happy New Year, I greeted my wife.
Now, there was a reply.
Happy New Year, I greeted my daughter.
Now, there was a reply.

Then,
I walked outside.
Happy New Year, I greeted
the tree,
the bird,
the hill,
the sun and the sky.
But, there was no reply.

Soon, I realized
In the universe, it's another day.
But, in the human world,
It's a New Year day.

Why, Why, Why?

Why should I accept my present?
'Cause my present is so dreadful.

Why shouldn't I dwell in my past?
'Cause my past was so wonderful.

Why shouldn't I hope for a future?
'Cause my present is so dreadful.

Virtual World Vs Real World

In the Virtual World,
You always have a present,
You always have a past,
You always have a future.

In the Real World,
You do not have a present,
You do not have a past,
You do not have a future.

In the Virtual World,
Everything is in your head.
In the Real World,
Everything is in front of your eyes.

Living In Both The Worlds

Living in both the worlds,
Dealing with both the worlds,
And keeping a distinction
Between both the worlds
Brings such a clarity
That no book, no teacher
Ever pointed out to me
when
I was searching for the Truth.

You Are Not
Who You Think You Are

You are not your name
'Cause name is a concept.
You are not a concept.

You are not your job
'Cause job is a concept.
You are not a concept.

You are not a spouse
'Cause spouse is a concept.
You are not a concept.

You are not a citizen
'Cause citizen is a concept.
You are not a concept.

You are not a human
'Cause human is a concept.
You are not a concept.

Whatever you can think of
is always a concept.
You are not a concept.

Hence,
You are not
who you think you are.

Real You

You are *not*
who you think you are.
'Cause what you think
is always Virtual.
But, you are, in fact, Real.

Real you is there
when you are free:
Free of your thoughts,
Free of your emotions,
Free of Your Virtual Self.

Real you is:
Who sees without a thought
Who hears without a thought
Who smells without a thought
Who tastes without a thought
Who senses without a thought.

Real you is always here,
in the Now, without a thought.

Hiding Behind----

Hiding behind
those clothes, jewelry and shoes,
Hiding behind
the curtains of your house,
Hiding behind
the steering wheel of your car,
Hiding behind
the glamour of your success, wealth and fame,
Hiding behind
the pity of your failure, poverty, and shame,
Hiding behind
your name and your grandiose family name,
Hiding behind
all of your ideas, concepts and emotions,
is
you.
Alas! That is not even Real You

Freedom From Your Virtual Self

No urge for self control
once, you are free of your Virtual Self.

No issues of self-esteem
once, you are free of your Virtual Self.

No need for self-improvement
once, you are free of your Virtual Self.

Self-righteousness dies out
once, you are free of your Virtual Self.

Selfishness cannot be
once, you are free of your Virtual Self.

Self pity does not exist
once, you are free of your Virtual Self.

But, what is Your Virtual Self?

Who you think you are
is Your Virtual Self.

"I" and I

"I" must find out
a cure for my illness
Or
"I"may die.
Hence, I tremble
and I cry.

Who is this "I"?
One day, I asked
as wisdom came by.

This "I" is the reason
Why I cry.
This "I" is not me
'cause it wasn't there
when I was born.

Once free of this "I"
I no longer tremble
and, I no longer cry!

A Life form, In Real!

I carry so many titles
a name,
a spouse,
a citizen,
a doctor,
a neighbor,
and a writer.

In Real, I am not
a name,
a spouse,
a citizen,
a doctor,
a neighbor,
and a writer.

In Real, I am a life form,
Like, every other life form.

Genie Is Out Of The Bottle

Why cannot Man see
the destruction, he is causing
to the fellow man,
to the fellow animals,
to the fellow plants
and
to his own sweet home.

Why cannot Man see
the flames of devastation,
the heat of devastation,
the floods of devastation
and
the disease of devastation.

Why is man so blind?
"Cause he has been hijacked
by the virtual "I"
that inhabits every mind.

The virtual "I" is always hungry
for
more power
more fame
more money
more entertainment.

The virtual "I" is like the Genie
that is out of the bottle.

I Am Going Nowhere

I am sitting right here.
I am going nowhere,
nowhere, nowhere, nowhere.

In the bliss of the Now,
I feel no pain,
I feel no fear,
I feel no lust,
I feel no love,
I feel no hate.

In the bliss of the Now,
I feel such a joy,
I feel such a peace.

That's why, my friend,
I am sitting right here.
I am going nowhere,
nowhere, nowhere, nowhere.

The Busy Mind

Have you ever watched your mind?
Full of thoughts
that swirl around
and never come to a stop.

All kinds of thoughts,
one after the other,
like a storm of bees,
stinging you all over.

Free yourself
from the web of thoughts.

Freed from the thoughts,
You live in peace
Mind gets in peace
Body gets in peace.
Peace that
a busy mind can't see.

Joy Of Living

My crazy days are over
as wisdom keeps on sinking.

I feel such peace inside me
there is no need for drinking.

No anger and no sadness
in the Now and present living.

I feel the joy of living
when, I am free of thinking.

Poor or Rich, It Really Does Not Matter

Born and raised in a poor home
without electricity or running water,
without a car, radio or television
I struggled between
happiness and sadness
love and hate
excitement and boredom
ego and jealousy
security and anxiety.

Climbing the rope of education
with a lot of pain and hard work
at last, I lived in a rich home
full of amenities of the modern world.
Yet,
I struggled between
happiness and sadness
love and hate
excitement and boredom
ego and jealousy
security and anxiety
Till
One day I woke up from the sleep.
Free of the virtual "I"
I am neither jealous nor embarrassed
Not judging good or bad
I am neither thrilled nor mad.

Not living in the past
I am neither happy nor sad.
Not living in the future
I am neither secure nor anxious.
Living in the Now
I am peaceful, content and joyful.

Poor or rich, it really does not matter
Asleep or awake, is what really does matter.

Space, Silence, Stillness

Objects cannot be without the Space.
Sounds cannot be without the Silence.
Movements cannot be without the Stillness.
Space, Silence, Stillness,
the canvas for the painting of the Universe.

Space, Silence, Stillness, Everywhere

You and I
Exist in space
Talk in silence
Walk in stillness.

We don't have to
Go to the orbit to be in space
Go to the to the cave to talk in silence
Go to the mountain to walk in stillness.

Space, silence, stillness
Is inside you and inside me
And out there, everywhere.

Self Realization

Awareness of the Now
Calmed the busy mind.
Now I can see,
the space out there,
emanating from here,
from inside me.
I feel the shear joy
I feel the real peace
All inside me.

Who is this me?
Asks the tricky mind.
No need to answer,
'Cause no words can see
What's real me.

You can also be
free of your mind.
Only then you can see
the true who are
which no words can ever see.

All of You, Tickle My Heart

White light,
Shimmering on the water,
in a never ending
whirls and loops.

White flowers,
dancing in the wind.

Tiny bubbles,
playing on the water.

Green trees,
swinging back and forth.

Yellow light,
shining through the leaves.

Yellow sun,
looking through the haze.

All of you, tickle my heart!

In the Real Now

In the Real Now,
there is no name
there is no Thought,
there is no Emotion.
not even love or compassion.

But,
A spacious vastness
And all the objects in it.
An utter silence
And all the sounds in it.
A profound stillness
And all the movements in it.

Space, silence, stillness
That, words can never know.

In the Conceptual Now

In the Conceptual Now,
You have a name,
You have a job,
You have a house,
You have a spouse,
You have a mission,
You may be wealthy,
You may be healthy,
You may be happy,
You may be famous.

Or

You may *not* have a job,
You may *not* have a house,
You may *not* have a spouse,
You may *not* have a mission,
You may *not* be wealthy,
You may *not* be healthy,
You may *not* be happy,
You may *not* be famous.

In the Conceptual Now
You are stuck in your thoughts,
You are full of your emotions,
You stay in your mind.
You do not see the space
And all the objects in it.
You do not hear the silence
And all the sounds in it.
You do not sense the stillness
And all the movements in it.

The Now

With the blazing torch of logic
look at the prison of the Past and the Future.

Where does the Past lives, have you ever wondered?
Where does the Future lives, have you ever wondered?

Both are the creation of your mind, and no more.
In fact, there is only Now, and no more.

You call it a moment, but in Real
It expands beyond the limits of the Beginning and the Ending.

Whether it is Mars, Moon or the Big dipper,
All stars roam around in the Now.

The Moon travels through the sky, immersed in the Now,
It rises in the Now, and it sets in the Now.

With the shower of red, orange and yellow rays,
The sun rises again and again, in the Now.

The gentle breeze travels, in the Now.
The dark thunderous clouds travel, in the Now.

The gusty wind also travels in the Now.
The rain drops also fall in the Now.

The rapids of the river flow as the rooster crows,
Two swans flow down the river, in the Now.

The peaks of the hill stand tall and still.
The nightingale sings her songs, in the Now.

On the soft, still carpet of the lake,
Ducks flow smoothly, carefree, in the Now

Butterflies flutter around in the courtyard, full of flowers,
Sweet fragrance soaks the air, in the Now.

The picturesque chase between the sunlight and the shades,
The yellow and orange clouds float, in the Now.

The water swirls around with ecstasy to kiss the sand,
The spreading waves of the ocean travel, in the Now.

I came from behind and softly kissed my wife's lips.
I feel intense heat of pleasure, in the Now.

Everyone is born, in the Now
and
Everyone dies in the Now.

Nothing can ever happen, outside the Now.
The entire universe exists in the Now.

See the effect of the transparent rays of the Now,
The fog of all worries starts to dissipate.

See the effect of the sacred lap of the Now,
The worries of tomorrow start to die out.

Oh! look carefully, who is coming down here,
Wearing a colorful dress of the past and the future.

It will misguide you and take you back
Into the prison of the past, and the worries of the future.

You are listening to the sound of the Truth, in the Now
Break down the chains of the past and the future, right Now.

Dancing With Ecstasy

I am dancing with ecstasy,
ever since I realized You.
Now I am drunk,
without having any drink.

I am dancing in the fire of ecstasy.
My shadow is also dancing with me.
The flame is also dancing with me,
bold sometimes, and shy at others.

On the horizon, I see the rays of the sunrise.
I see the intense play of the bright colors.
The rising sun talks to me
and whispers the secret of ecstasy.

I see You in the day, and I see You at night.
I see You at dawn, and I see You at dusk.
I see You in the still air,
and in the colors of the rainbow.

I see You in the dance of the peacock.
I see You in the songs of the nightingale.
When I smell the fragrance of the flower
I realize You live in Everything.

You are in the tree, You are in the fire.
You are in the rapids of a running river.
When I see the snow flakes falling
My heart quivers with ecstasy.

You are in the mountain, You are in the cave,
You are in the stillness of the lake.
The playful assembly of the stars
is there only because of You.

There is no path, and there is no destination
that leads to Your house.
'Cause You are everywhere,
not confined to a house.

I see no Muslims, and no Hindus
and no Christians either.
Everyone is Your Manifestation
Hence, there is no reason to fight.

I look into my heart, I see You.
In the movement of my breath, I see You.
I am voicing because of You,
whatever You enable me to voice.

Theater Of Life

In the theater of life,
can you wake up, and see
the show of life,
playing in the Now.

Sadly, most of us,
sleep through the show.
Dreaming of "What if "
Dreaming of "What should"
Dreaming of "What could."

The show of life
simply goes on.
When time comes
for you to move on.
You panic, and you cry.
You don't want to die.
You want to live on
in the theater of life.
Not to watch the show,
but to sleep some more.

A Dialogue Between The Mind And The Heart

The Mind Says:

Before I took man into my strong arms,
he used to live in the cold dark caves.

I tamed him into the confines of civilization.
I bestowed upon him the fountain of knowledge.

Then, I blessed him with so many machines.
Now, he lives in comfort, without shedding a sweat.

Just with the movement of the tip of a finger,
he can get rid of all the darkness of the night.

No one comes close to his speed of flying.
He can travel a thousand miles in a blink of the eye.

Without taking a single step, he is connected to everyone.
While sitting in his house, he knows what happened in the world.

He moved from the caves to the villages, and then into the cities.
Only because of me, he has reached the moon and the stars.

The Heart Replies:

In the name of civilization and knowledge,
You slowly molded man into your slave.

Then, you divided mankind into thousand pieces,
in the name of race, religion and nation.

You taught him how to fight in all possible ways.
You equipped him with the piles and piles of weaponry.

For this reason, he remains afraid of each other.
For this reason, he is lost in the cycle of "war and peace."

He got trapped in the desire of "wanting more."
Thanks to your lure, his content is gone, forever.

He got so immersed in the knowledge you invented,
that, he cannot even see while the light is all around him.

Intoxicated in the mental bar you created,
now he keeps destroying his own sweet home.

All of the industries you graciously invented,
keep raising the temperature of his sweet home.

You invented the concepts of the past and the future.
Now man stays lost in the web of the past and the future.

The grievances of the past keep stinging him, forever.
He keeps burning in the fire of hate and anger.

He knows no inner peace, even for a moment,
'cause he is always restless with the worries of the future.

Before the colorful *illusions* of your magic,
this man used to live in heaven.

He had no sorrows, he had no worries.
From dawn till dusk, he used to live in joy.

Immersed in the bliss of the "Now",
he used to play and stay in ecstasy.

Free of the long, dark shadows of greed and fear,
he was content, and he had no worries.

He greeted everyone, without any selfish motives,
'cause, he had no friends and had no foes.

The fire of hate was not burning in his heart,
'cause the fire-pit of the past didn't exist, yet.

No one was pretty and no one was ugly,
'cause the concept of beauty didn't exist, yet.

No one was sick and no one was old.
No one ever died of the fear of dying.

Free of all the concepts, he used to stay in bliss.
Yes, this man used to live in heaven, once.

Change The World

So,
You want to change the world.
But, so do I.

You want to change me.
I want to change you.
And that's why we fight.

We want to change the world
according to our wishes.
And that's why we fight.

But, if there is no me,
and there is no you.
Then, there is no need,
to change the world.

So Close, But So Far

"See, we are
one generation away
from
getting rid of prejudice,
getting rid of hate
and
achieving the world peace."

"My friend,
We will continue to be
one generation away
from
getting rid of prejudice,
getting rid of hate
and
achieving the world peace."

Possessions

Nothing is mine
and
Nothing is yours.

But, you think
Everything is yours.

Money is yours
and
Car is yours.

House is yours
and
Cat is yours.

Horse is yours
and
Dog is yours.

Boy is yours
and
Girl is yours.

Wife is yours
and
Maid is yours.

Food is yours
and
Land is yours.

Church is yours
and
Temple is yours.

Life is yours
and
Body is yours.

Earth is yours
and
Universe is yours.

Birth is yours
and
Death is yours.

God is yours
and
Om is yours.

Lost in the dream,
You think as if
Everything is yours.

Wake up and See
With the wide open eyes.

Nothing is yours
and
Nothing is mine.

I am not yours
and
You are not mine.

Doing, Doing, Doing, Doing

Doing, doing, doing, doing
You always keep on doing.

You wake up in the morning
And start your list of doing.
All day long, you are doing.

You do it through the evening.
You do it through the night.
You simply keep on doing.

Exhausted in the morning
You start your list of doing,
A list that has no ending.
Like a *mindless* little hamster
On a tiny plastic wheel
That always keeps on spinning.

All Present In My Chest

Golden light on the west,
pink light on the east
and
a sliver of yellow moon
in the umbrella of the blue sky.

A very quiet mountain.
A strong wind
sings through the dancing trees.

Water drops
dribble, dribble, dribble.

I walk, walk, walk,
using these legs,
using these eyes
and ears as well.

I
see all of the Space,
hear all of the Silence,
feel all of the Stillness.

I sense
a sense of inner Space
a sense of inner Peace,
a sense of inner Stillness,
so utterly emotion-free,
all present in my chest.

A wave of joy
spreads through the arms,
spreads through the legs
and the rest of this body.

A black and white cat
runs here and runs there,
pounces up and down a tree.
Cute, but not in peace,
hyper, but not joyful,
looks anxious in his eyes.

Now, it got more dark.
All the sky is dusky blue.
A bright star shows up
not far from the moon.

I sit on the ground,
watch the quiet mountain,
hear the singing wind,
and the dribbling water drops.

Still, I
see all of the Space,
hear all of the Silence,
feel all of the Stillness

Still, I sense
a sense of inner Space
a sense of inner Peace
a sense of inner Stillness,
so utterly emotion-free,
All present in my chest.

Eternal Peace

Sun, shining on my face.
Feeling of warmth,
That is so great!

Strong wind,
whistling through the trees.

Clunky sound
of the old washing machine.

Laying here,
I feel the silence, in between.

Suddenly, a rush of warmth
runs through my every corner
and in between.

AAh!
I no longer exist
in the noisy, busy mind.
I just came back
to the eternal peace of God.

Everything Simply Is!

Moon is not yours,
Moon is not mine,
Moon is moon.

Sun is not yours,
Sun is not mine,
Sun is sun.

Space is not yours,
Space is not mine,
Space is space.

Sea is not yours,
Sea is not mine,
Sea is sea.

Land is not yours,
Land is not mine,
land is land.

God is not yours,
God is not mine,
God is God.

Wake up, and see
Nothing is yours
and nothing is mine.
Everything simply is!

No Friends-No Enemies

Sun is spreading
its warmth
to everyone
'cause it has no friends
and
it has no enemies.

You will have no enemies
only
if you have no friends.

In Sync With Nature, Are You?

In Sync with Nature,
Are you?

How wasteful really are you,
How greedy really are you,
How dreadful really are you,
How fearful really are you,
How hateful really are you,
How pitiful really are you,
How cunning really are you
How loving really are you,
How sinful really are you,
How noble really are you,
How happy really are you,
How hurtful really are you,

Wake up and see it yourself,
NOT, in sync with nature are you.

What's Life

Your job is not your Life.
Your goal is not your Life.
Your house is not your Life.
Your spouse is not your Life.

It is not your ideas,
beliefs or traditions.
It is not your past,
nor is it your future.
It is not your health,
nor is it your wealth.

It is not your success,
your failure, or your mess.
your birth, or your death.
Your body, as well
is simply not your life.

What you think is your life,
in fact, is *not* your life,
'cause life is like a river
that continues to flow
and never ever dries up.

Like a fish in the river,
you live in this river,
the sacred river of life
which continues to flow
whether you live
or
whether you die.

Life Goes On

One day, You will die
and I will die
but, life goes on.

Every life form
does come to an end,
but, life goes on.

Free of the law
of birth and death,
life goes on.

You are life,
you are a form.
I am life,
I am a form.
Form does die,
But, life goes on.

In this way,
one day, you will die
one day, I will die,
but,
you and I will never ever die.

Entry - Exit

I enter this world
Without a passport, airplane, boat or a bus
Without any clothes, money, house or a car
Without any name, religion, foes or friends
Without any language, concepts or ideas
and no emotions either.
And
I exit this world
Without a passport, airplane, boat or a bus
Without any clothes, money, house, or a car
Without any name, religion, foes or friends
Without any language, concepts or ideas,
But,
soiled with tons and tons of emotions.

My Illness

Stuck in a lingering illness,
I lived in a rusty cage.

The more I tried to evade,
the narrower got the cage.

Thinking of "What may"
and "What if"
I trembled in fear.

My heart was pounding,
my throat was closing,
I was gasping for air.

In the jaws of dread and fear
I let go of the busy mind.

Then, I saw myself, seeing
what's real, and what's here,
in front of my eyes,
not in my busy mind.

Soon, I realized
one day I die,
no matter how much I try.
So, why worry for something
I can never deny.

Right then, rolled in an inner peace,
a different kind of peace,
I never saw before.

Immersed in this peace,
I listened to the silence

while laying in my bed.
No fear and No worry,
I felt so blessed.

Now, I live my daily life,
accepting what it brings.
The pain, and the joy,
one comes in as
the other goes by.

Now I feel
What's inside Me
is out there as well.

Now,
I see the diving birds,
the dancing leaves and trees,
the icicles, hanging down
from the brim
of a frozen fountain.

This constant play of Nature
stirs up waves of joy.
No longer do I cry.
I simply enjoy.
The joy of being here
The joy of Real "Me"
free of any scare.

Castration: Dog's Point of View

I see my human father
and my human mother,
get down on knees and elbows
to make some human babies.

But, I do not have desire
to make my little puppies.
I wonder what has happened,
why I do not have desire
to make my little puppies.

Doggy Shrink

You give me cans of food
that, I simply cannot eat.
You call a doggy shrink
who doesn't know my things.
Pause, and think for yourself:
you buy these cans of food
that has my name and picture,
and a lot of healthy claims
but, its not my *real* food.
In case, you have forgotten
In real, I am a dog
and
meat is my real food.

The Stupid Fences, Chains And Humans

At last, I see another dog.
I run to lick her face,
' cause, I am getting tired
to lick the human face.

I want to get together.
But,
there is this stupid fence.

Ahh!
I see a little gap
underneath the stupid fence.
Dig, dig and keep on digging.
Now hole is big enough,
for me to slip my body
underneath the stupid fence.

We smell and lick each other,
we run and chase each other
and, chase some goofy bunnies.

But,
there comes my angry owner,
embarrassed of my actions.
He puts this stupid chain
on my fluffy neck, and
drags me back to my prison,
far away from the heaven
of me and my fuzzy buddy.

Then, one day my human father
takes me to a wide open space,
where I meet so many dogs
and, no one is on a chain.

I run and play and play
with every dog in this heaven.

What's wrong with the humans?
They love these chains and fences.
They don't know how to play
with every other human.

Lady And Her Dog

You do it in the backyard.
You do it in the park.
You do it in the street
and
also on the beach.

In front of little children,
in front of modest ladies,
in front of older folks,
in front of other dogs.

You *sinful* little creature,
you bring me such a shame.

A trip to veterinarian
with a bill of ninety-nine
and you will get in line.

Bird and I

Searching for your food,
I see you soaring high
on the tides of gusty wind.

I see you simply perch on
any fence, roof or tree.
Oh my God! you are free!

You drink from any pot,
lake, river or a stream.
You eat from any tree.
Oh my God! you are free!

You have no house to sleep.
You sleep, when you get sleepy
on a mountain, hilltop or tree.
Oh my God! you are free!

You are not afraid of thieves
"cause, you carry no possessions.
Oh my God! you are free!

You mate with other birds
when time is ripe for you
to reproduce and carry on
the basic purpose of life.

You build a tiny nest
with days of hardy work
and a lot of tiny sticks
for the newborn tender chicks.

You guard the newborn chicks
from any kind of threat

that arises in front of you,
but not inside your head.

You feed the hungry babies.
You teach them how to fly.

One day, they choose to fly.
They fly, fly and fly
without saying you goodbye
and you don't even cry.

Oh my God! you are free!
Free of any stress
though, you surely carry on
a busy, hectic life.

Man And The Bird

You come in my backyard
and eat away the food
I put for my dog.

I see you sitting on the fence
and making out
with your chirping noisy friends.

Then, you fly into my trees
to make out some more
with your chirping, noisy friends.

You and your friends
eat away my precious fruit.
You, selfish little creature.
No respect for what's mine.
No respect for my fences.
No respect for my emotions.
No respect for my beliefs.

Wait, till I get a clever trap
Then, I will teach you little birdie,
What's yours and what's mine.

Baby, It's All Fine!

So baby, you got pregnant.
You don't know what to do.
Afraid of this and that,
you often stay so sad.

Just pause, and look around.
In Nature, birds and trees,
wolves, tigers, bears and bees,
once, reach their healthy peak,
they simply try to reproduce.

Because,
This is the law of Nature.

So,
Relax and get in touch
with your inner peace.

After all,
you haven't done a crime.

You did what every form
does it to carry on
the basic purpose of life.

True, Unconditioned Love

Unconditioned love
does not know
what is yours
and
what is mine.

Free from division,
it knows no fear.
Free from fear,
no need to defend
my concepts and possessions.

No wishing for the praise,
'cause it is not afraid.
No need to compromise.
No need for give and take.

True, unconditioned love
rises itself,
once I am free
of my conditioned mind.

Then,
I simply start to see
"I in you"
And
"You in me "

What _Really_ Causes Hate?

Hate has many faces
and
it has many forms.

You get stuck on all the details
about its faces and its forms.

Wrapped up in your emotions
you cause a lot of harm.

You see it in the others
But, _not_ in your self.

Thus,
Hate, skillfully thrives in hiding
in you, and every one else.

Can
you rise above the details
and
rise above your emotions
to
see what <u>really</u> causes hate?

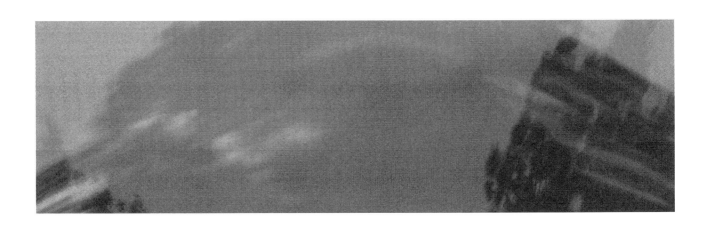

Fire Of History

Can you burn down
the fire of history.
The fire that breeds
hate and rivalry.
The fire that divides
man from man.

The fire that propels
the need to protect,
the need to defend,
the need to control,
the need to fight.

The fire of history
is burning down
the entire mankind
in the flames of hate,
in the flames of revenge.

The flames that engulf
the entire mankind.

It Is Such A Shame

You can't stop the hate
till you stop the race
for the power,
for the money,
for the sex,
for the fame.

It is such a shame.
we all keep fighting
for the power,
for the money,
for the sex,
for the fame,
even when we have
a lot of power, money, sex and fame.
It is such a shame.

Perpetual Fighting

Everyone is wishing hard
to end the deadly war.
But, everyone is fighting,
everyone, is at war.

I see at the home.
I see it on the road.
I see it in the school.
I see it in the office.
I see it in the court.
I see it in the town.

Some fight to win a trophy.
Some fight to make a point.
Some fight to get more power.
Some fight to get more money.

To win at every cost
is the mantra we inhabit.

But, here is no real winner,
for, someone has to lose
for someone else to win.

Despite this law of logic
Man simply keeps on fighting.

Why???

'Cause he is so divided.
divided into nations,
divided into races.
divided into cultures,
religions and traditions.

Division is the reason
why everyone's at war
why everyone is fighting
And
will always keep on fighting.

Upbringing

I was peaceful
before you taught me
what peace is.

I was joyful
before you taught me
what joy is.

I was fearless
before you taught me
what courage is.

I was free
before you taught me
what freedom is.

Thank you "upbringing,"
now, I know it all,
but, have <u>none</u>.

Robot

You love some days
'cause you are told to do.
You hate some days
'cause you are told to do.

You love some people
'cause you are told to do.
You hate some people
'cause you are told to do.

You try to be nice
'cause you are told to do.
You love to fight
'cause you are told to do.

You try to win
'cause you are told to do.
You hate to lose
'cause you are told to do.

You feel so proud
'cause you are told to do.
You feel so humble
'cause you are told to do.

Don't live in the past
chat you are told to do.
Don't worry about future
what you are told to do.

You *try* to do
what you are told to do.
Like a robot, you do
what you are told to do.

No One Is Free!

Your are not free
until
you are free of the shackles,
the shackles of:
hate and revenge,
greed and fear,
thrill and excitement,
compulsion and compassion,
embarrassment and shame,
envy and jealousy,
guilt and sadness,
anger and madness.

Now can you see
why no one is free!

Mine?

Butterflies,
Yellow, black and white,
sucking away
the nectar of life
from the flowers that I own.
How rude, and how selfish
these butterflies really are.

Birds,
Yellow, black and white,
very noisy as they fly,
from tree to tree to tree
and wake me up
from my early morning sleep.

"Get out of my trees
you nasty little beasts."
How rude, and how selfish,
these birds really are.

Bunnies,
with their cute little feet,
hop over my lush green field,
eat away those tender veggies,
the veggies that I own.
How rude, and how selfish,
these bunnies really are.

Squirrels,
and those pesky birds,
eat away the juicy fruits,
the fruits that I own.
How rude, and how selfish,
these squirrels and birds are.

Lost in my painful thoughts
I kept on feeling mad
till
I felt the morning sun,
tap on my naked back,
with gentle hand of warmth.

I woke up from the dream
to see the light and the warmth,
the sun is shining on
every bird and every tree,
butterfly, bunny and me.

Wow!
In Nature,
you do *not* own a thing,
you eat up what you see,
you eat up other lives,
so life can carry on
its journey through its forms.

In The Name Of Evolution

I am a total witness
to my own evolution,
'cause,
I lived through all the phases
of the evolution of the man.

I started my long journey
in waters, yes in waters,
in the warm and cozy waters
of the womb of my own mother.

I started as a single cell
which kept on replicating.
I kept on getting bigger.

Once,
I used to look like tadpole,
I used to look like fish
and other forms of life,
forms that still exist
in the waters of the ocean.

But,
I kept on replicating
and kept on getting bigger
till I was what you call
a tiny little human
in the waters of my mother,
in the waters of the ocean.

Then,
One day, for some reason
I had to leave the waters.
The waters of the womb

The waters of the ocean.

I landed on the land.
Discomfort was just too much.
I screamed out real loud.
I cried and cried and cried
but, soon I realized,
I need to find some food
to feed my hunger down.

I struggled, and I struggled.
I struggled very hard
But, never did I give up.

First I could only lay
and lay and lay and lay.
But,
I kept on working hard
till I could move a yard.

I never ever quit
then I was fit to sit.

I kept on working hard
till I could simply crawl
and stand- and at last,
I could even walk.

Eat, drink and go to sleep,
I got it all together.
I lived in such a bliss
No fear, greed or anger,
In heaven sure, I lived.

Then,
I got a little clever,
Invented basic tools

that helped me get my food.

Then,
We humans grew in number,
We started living in groups,
to survive against those animals
that loved to eat us all up.

With the dawn of civilization,
everyone would get a name,
a label meant to find out
each and every one of us
who lived in a human group.

This was the birth of "I"
the virtual, unreal "I."

We humans did more thinking,
invented some more concepts.
we came up with some rules
for everyone to live
in order and in peace.

But,
concepts would keep on growing.
Technology and the concepts
slowly took us over.

The virtual lines of concepts
divided all the humans
into tribes, races and religions.

Division led to fear,
which led to nasty fighting.
In fighting, we are always
protecting our possessions,
ideas, beliefs and concepts.

In fighting we are killing
our fellow human beings.

In fear now we shiver,
we don't have any peace.
In heaven, we are no more,
we live a hellish life!
A heavy price we paid
in the name of evolution.

But,
it is the evolution
that blessed us with a sense,
we call it common sense.
Alas! we seldom use it,
'cause we are always knee deep
in the filthy mud of concepts.

Fog Of Concepts

When I set aside
what I was told
since my childhood
till I was old.

Then, I saw
no friends, no foes
no boss, no workers
no neighbors, no strangers.

I did not see
any Jews or Muslims
any Hindus or Christians
any French or English
any Italians or Iranians
any Latinos or Wasps
any Arabs or Armenians.

What I saw
Everyone is a human
Everyone is a life-form
But,
lost in the *fog* of concepts.

Dual Nature Of Concepts

With love,
You keep hate alive.

With peace,
You keep war alive.

With friendship,
You keep animosity alive.

With happiness,
You keep sadness alive.

With success,
You keep failure alive.

With beauty,
You keep ugliness alive.

With nobility,
You keep evil alive.

With God,
You keep devil alive.

Stuck in the concepts,
lost you are
for ever and ever!

A Variety Of Concepts

Some concepts are necessary
for society to be functional.

Some concepts are unnecessary
But, people remain in their prison.

Some concepts are absurd
and make society dysfunctional.

Some concepts are harmful
to yourself and the others.

Can you *not* follow those concepts
that are unnecessary, absurd and harmful.

Nature Is Always Nude

Lion is nude, Tiger is nude,
Cow is nude, Crow is nude.
Cat is nude, Bat is nude.
Bird is nude,
so is the Dog and the Frog.

Nature is always nude.

Nude were you born
and
Nude was I was born.

Then,
You were hid in clothes,
I was hid in clothes.
Everyone is hid in clothes.

We all were then told,
it is bad to be nude.
Shame on you, if you are nude.
Sinful are you, if you are nude.

In the haze of modesty,
In the maze of morality,
we, humans are so lost
forever and forever!

But truth is always nude,
Nature is always nude.

Wrapped Up In The Concepts

Sit my friend and see,
what you see in Nature
with the very eyes of yours.

Everyone is naked
and free,
except for you and me.

Naked were we born.
But,
we got covered by the clothes
and
wrapped up in the concepts.

Concept of nudity,
Concept of morality,
Concept of beauty,
Concept of modesty.

In the prison of the concepts,
we shiver with the fear,
we shiver with the anger,
we shiver with the shame,
we shiver with the guilt.

Alas, we do not have a clue
what happened to us all.

We forgot, who we really are,
under the covers of the clothes,
under the layers of the concepts.

Judging Or Not

You judge me,
Because:
I am a teenager,
I am a parent,
I am a teacher,
I am a preacher,
I am a Christian,
I am a Muslim,
I am a Jew,
I am a Hindu,
I am an Atheist,
I am a Chinese,
I am a German,
I am a Japanese,
I am a French,
I am a Mexican,
I am an Indian,
I am a Leftist,
I am a Rightist.......

You *cannot* judge me,
If
I am not a teenager,
I am not a parent,
I am not a teacher,
I am not a preacher,
I am not a Christian,
I am not a Muslim,
I am not a Jew,
I am not a Hindu,
I am not an Atheist,
I am not a Chinese,
I am not a German,
I am not a Japanese,

I am not a French,
I am not a Mexican,
I am not an Indian,
I am not a Leftist,
I am not a Rightist…….

Two Sides Of The Same Coin

Why does love change into hate?
Because these are two sides of the same coin.

Why does non-violence change into violence?
Because these are two sides of the same coin.

Why does friendship change into animosity?
Because these are two sides of the same coin.

Why does beauty change into ugliness?
Because these are two sides of the same coin.

Why does wealth changes into poverty?
Because these are two sides of the same coin

Why does health changes into disease?
Because these are two sides of the same coin

Why does birth changes into death?
Because these are two sides of the same coin

In the revolving door of concepts,
You stay lost, confused and upset.

What Is Common Sense?

Common Sense is
what you use
rarely, barely, scarcely.

You don't learn it in a school.
You are born with this tool.
A priceless functional tool,
You hardly ever use,
'Cause you stay stuck
In your busy mind,
A very busy mind
Full of knowledge and the concepts
You acquire in a school.

Common sense is
when you are free:
Free of
the knowledge and the notions,
the habits and emotions,
the bondage and devotions,
the concepts and commotions.

Naked, Naked, Naked

Naked, naked, naked.
Naked, naked, naked.
You were naked, I was naked
We all were naked.
When we were born.

Naked of the concepts.
Naked of the knowledge.
Naked of emotions.
Naked of commotions.
When we were born.

No burden of the past.
No worries of tomorrow.
No pressure of society.
No need for any judging.
When we were born.

No one was in the rage.
No one was in the race.
No one was feeling sad.
No one was feeling mad.
When we were born.

We all lived in a peace.
We all lived in a rhythm.
We all lived in the Now.
We all lived in a heaven.
When we were born.

Then came a wicked monster.
Tricked us into concepts.
Wrapped all us in the clothes.
Wrapped all us in the concepts.

We aren't naked now.

Afraid of being nude.
Afraid of being rude.
Afraid of being late.
Afraid of being laid.
Afraid of being caught.
Afraid of being lost.
Afraid of being sad.
Afraid of being mad.
Afraid of our foe.
Afraid of our death.
We shiver and we cry.
All covered by the concepts
We aren't naked now.

Divided we all are.
Blinded we all are.
Greedy we all are.
Jealous we all are.
Judging we all are.
Grudging we all are.
Hateful we all are.
Shameful we all are.
Grateful we all are.
Blameful we all are.
Pressured we all are.
Tethered we all are.
All covered by the concepts.
We aren't naked now.

In the maze of all the concepts
Lost, surely we all are.
All covered by the clothes.
All covered by the concepts.
We aren't naked now.

If You Dare

If you dare
to see with the eyes
that do not judge at all.

You see
No roses, no lilies
No mums, no daisies
No apples, no cherries
No melons, no berries.

You see
No Muslims, no Hindus
No Christians, no Jews
No Germans, no Russians
No Irish, no Indians.

You simply realize,
no one is really what
your mind is trained to think.

Without the goggles of the concepts,
you see it very clear,
you see it what is Real.

All you see, is this vastness
and
forms of different shapes
and
forms of different colors
and
all are simply lit up
with the same lamp of Life.

Memories!

Bad memories
Oh! Bad memories.
They beat me down,
They thrash me around.
I want to run away,
to a far, far land.
But like a wild beast,
they chase me down.
until I am
really, really down.

I try to fight away
This beast of the wild.
I try to train it,
I try to change it,
I try to rationalize,
Just to find myself,
in a total paralyze.

Stuck in the past,
I sob and I cry.
A prison for life
and no way out
No matter how much I
try, try, try.

I also latch on
to the sweet memories.
An escape for a while,
but soon I realize
They are gone for a while.

I get very sad.
I sob and I cry,

A prison for life,
and no way out.
No matter how much I
try, try, try.

The Deception Of Time

Have you ever wondered
What is this thing we call time?
It does not even exist
With logic you can see.

Whatever happened Yesterday
is dead now.
Then, why is it alive Today.
Whatever may happen Tomorrow
You can never ever know.

What is this thing we call time.
It is an illusion,
With logic you can see.

Time is a creation of mind
and
mind is trapped in it.

In the prison of time,
You tremble day and night.
In the deception of time
You wander all your life.

If you want to see Reality,
Get out of the prison of time.
You are in touch with God
Once you are free of time.

How Long!

How long will you stay
in the rut of every day?
How long will you stay
in your own ways?
How long will you stay
in the room of your friends?
How long will you stay
mad at the ugly past?
How long will you stay
afraid of this and that?
How long will you stay
stuck in your own rights?
How long will you stay
in the prison of traditions?
How long will you stay
in the grip of expectations?
How long will you stay
in the dream of holidays?
How long will you stay
in the chase of your fame?
How long will you stay
lost in the human world?
That is not even Real.

How long will you play
the game of love and hate?
How long will you play
the game of win and lose?
How long will you play
the game of good and bad?
How long will you play
the game of war and peace?
How long will you play
the game of life and death?

The life that doesn't die.

How long will you hide
in the cloud of internet?
How long will you hide
in the glory of your past?
How long will you hide
in the heap of your medals?
How long will you hide
in the layers of your clothes?
How long will you hide
in the retreats of your beliefs?
How long will you hide
in the maze of noble missions?
How long will you hide
in the race of pure greed?
How long will you hide
in the heap of your possessions?
How long will you hide
in the pit of guilt and shame?
How long will you hide
in the fog of deadly drugs?
How long will you hide
in the ghost of your "I"?
That is not even Real.

Please, Tell me
How long, how long, how long
how long?

Enslaved

Enslaved by habits,
Enslaved by traditions,
Enslaved by culture,
Enslaved by religion,
Enslaved by nationalism,
Enslaved by capitalism,
Enslaved by socialism,
Enslaved by communism,
Enslaved by ego,
Enslaved by greed,
Enslaved by past,
Enslaved by future,

We remain stuck
in the prison of hate,
in the prison of fear,
in the prison of guilt,
in the prison of shame,
All in the name of
habits and traditions,
culture and religion,
This *ism* and that *ism.*

We stay in a rut
'Cause we don't have the guts
to be free:
free of habits,
free of traditions,
free of culture,
free of religion,
free of this *ism*
and
free of that *ism*.

Freedom From Tradition

May I humbly ask,
why do you celebrate,
Deewali, Eid or Christmas
And all of the national days?

You tell me,
"It's simply a tradition,
that has been passing down
from generation to generation."

But,
don't these old traditions,
divide a group of humans
from another group of humans.

Divided humans, then fight
in the name of God and Nations.

To bridge up these divisions
Can you be free from traditions?
A question, for you to answer,
A question, only you can answer.

Sacred Union

Ahh!
Your wide, inviting eyes
go deep into my soul.

I see my body boiling.
I see your body boiling.

The juice of your lip
I sip and sip and sip.

I touch with tender fingers
the back of your neck,
those silky, shimmering hair
and rounded, bulging breasts.

I see, I can't resist,
I see, you can't resist
the rising tide of fire
that melts down all the fear
and hang-ups, we inhabit
against
the natural force of sex.

I see our boiling bodies
merge into one another.
I see my self dissolving,
I see your self dissolving.

Now, you do not exist,
Now, I do not exist,
our souls are now united.

Uniting of two souls
is sacred to the Whole.

The Whole is simply dancing
The cosmos are rejoicing
this very sacred union,
which gives birth to a child.

With the birth of little child
This very sacred union
can never be *untied*.

You Are My Viagra

At
the falls of Niagara
You are my Viagra.

Bright colors of rainbow
stirs up my sexual flow.

In the thick of the mist
I start to kiss your lip.

I feel your body heat
under the drippy pants.

Like the thunder of the falls
I want to blast in you.

Stop,
We can't do this act of nature
in the sacred stillness of nature,
though all of the other animals
do the sacred act of nature
in the bliss of heavenly nature.

What's wrong with us, we humans
got opposed to the act of nature
in the bliss of heavenly nature.

You Are My Booster

I am the rooster
You are my booster.

Dancing in circles,
Chanting it louder,
You are my booster,
You are my booster.

I like to chase you
So,
I can embrace you
'Cause
You are my booster,
You are my booster.

I like to hug you,
I like to love you
'Cause
You are my booster,
You are my booster.

I like to feed you,
I like to keep you
'Cause
You are my booster
You are my booster.

I like that you and me
With all of our off-springs,
Dancing in circles,
Chanting it louder,
You are my booster,
You are my booster.

My Wife

Playing with your hair
I caress your tender ear.

Touching your cheeks and lips
with my shivering finger tips.

A storm rises inside me.
a storm of warmth,
a storm of pleasure,
a storm of excitement,
against
the background of stillness,
which is always here.

The Bush

Being in the bush,
I am
living in the bush.
I am
Happy in the bush.
I am
digging in the bush.
I am
sipping juices in the bush.
I am
growing fatter in the bush.
I am
going faster in the bush.
I am
exploding in the bush.
I am
watering thirsty bush.
I am
planting seeds in the bush.

Now
I am done, doing what
I was born to do.
To perpetuate life.

Soul To Soul

I am my soul,
You are your soul,
We are soul-mate
but, we are separate
in this life
and the life after death.

When I look into your eyes
I see your soul
looking at me
with love and passion.

When I look into your eyes
I see your soul
looking at me
with anger and hate.

When I look into your eyes
I see your soul
looking at me
with fear and sadness.

When I look into the eyes
of a newborn baby,
I see her soul
looking at me
with no emotions
but a deep, still, peace
which resonates with
the deep, still, peace
of my very own soul.

Stillness

Looking at the painting
of Nature in motion,
that the sun is drawing,
with the help of the clouds,
with the help of the trees,
with the help of the mountains,
All immersed in stillness,
Resonating with the stillness,
that is inside me.

It brings out a joy,
that runs through me.

Now painting has changed.
All there is dark,
nothing else to see.
But I still feel,
the stillness out there
and
inside me.

Joy Of Being, Joy Of Being

Shut your eyes,
and watch your breathing.
Mind gets calm
and heart starts feeling,
Joy of Being, Joy of Being.

Bird is singing,
Wind is ringing,
Train is whistling,
and heart is singing,
Joy of Being, Joy of Being

Open your eyes,
and watch your breathing.
Mind gets calm
and heart starts feeling,
Joy of Being, Joy of Being.

Sun is shining,
Clouds are flying
Tree is swinging,
Waves are twirling,
and flowers are smiling,
Joy of Being, Joy of Being.

The Movie Of Life

Looking through a window,
I see a diving bird,
A lot of dancing trees,
Flowers, that are smiling,
Mountains, that are sleeping,
Clouds, that are chasing
the sun up and down.

What a joyful movie,
the wonderful movie of life.

Then, I wonder
Who is really watching
this wonderful movie of life?

A wave of ecstasy
surges up, and runs through
this wonderful body of life.

Immersed in the bliss,
I am quiet, and I am still
And now, I can see
I am also part
of this wonderful movie of life.

Rhythm Of Life

Free yourself,
from the prison of the past.
Don't be afraid,
of the ghost of tomorrow
'cause neither is real,
it simply disappears
in the light of the "Now."

"Now" is real!
"Now" is true!
"Now" is joy!

You feel this joy:
By rising and by falling,
with the flight of a bird.
By glowing with the glow
of a shiny sunrise.
By surfing up and down
the colors of a rainbow.
By dancing with the dancing
leaves of a tree.
By whistling with the whistle,
of a blowing harsh wind.
By giggling with the giggle
of a three years old.
By gazing in the eyes
of a loving soul mate.

You live in the Now,
no matter "what is."
No running from pain
or any unease.

Only such a soul knows
what true joy is!
'cause it is dancing all the time
with the Rhythm of Life.

Reality Is All Around You

Look up
and
look down.

Look to the right
and
look to the left.

Look all around you
and, inside you.

'Cause Reality is
all around you
and, inside you.

Sun And I

The enticing maid of sunrays
tiptoed into my bed room,
kissed my forehead
warmed up my eyes
and
set up a soft fire of love.

It is dancing and twirling,
it is kissing me all over,
It is getting deep inside me'
reaching out to the far corners.

Soft rays and warm rays,
play with me, and flirt with me,
spreading in every direction,
they are warming up my heart.

A fountain of joy springs up,
electrical waves start running
from head to my toes,
I feel the waves ofjoy.

For hours do I lay
in the cradle of this joy.
In the lap of sunny rays
I lay free, yes I do.

Party Of The Stars

What a scene I saw
when I woke up last night
to get a drink of water.

The stars were having a party.
They were talking to each other.
They were playing hide and seek
in the deep stillness of the moon.

Looking at this play,
my heart is opening up.
It's reaching out to the moon.
It's reaching out to the stars.

The moon and the stars
are not far any more.
I am in the party now,
playing hide and seek,
immersed in deep love.

Now,
the cool moon is in my heart,
the twinkling stars are in my heart.
The light is dancing inside me.
The light is dancing outside me.

The moon, the stars and this human
got enlightened from each other,
singing the song of true love,
touching the heart of each other
In the deep stillness of the night.

My House And Your House

Stuck in my house:
I was asleep,
I was scared,
I was mad,
I was sad.

One day,
I woke up from the deep sleep,
got outside the prison of my house.
Now, I see you everywhere.
I see you inside, I see you outside.

In your house:
Blue birds and yellow birds
sing their song at dawn.
Sun comes out
with the dazzling red rays
that penetrate deep in my soul.

I bath with the cold air.
I keep sitting under the tree.
The swinging branches swing in my heart.

The moth is flirting with the flower,
dipping in and sipping its juices.
The flower is dancing with joy.

Seeing all of this play of nature,
my heart is singing with joy.
my heart is dancing with joy.

I forgot my food, I forgot my body,
then, I realized real Me,
then, I realized real God.

Mr. Autumn Tree

Mr. Autumn tree,
Have you seen yourself
lately?

Have you compared yourself
with your picture
just a few months ago?

Pale are your leaves.
Slowly they die
and fall on the ground.

Aren't you afraid?
Piece by piece,
you may ultimately die.

Shouldn't you call a doctor
or surf the internet
to figure out your mess.

Relax my friend,
replied the autumn tree.
"I am who I am!
Free of what may,
in the Now I stay."

What Is Death?

You say, I die
when death comes by.
No, my friend,
I don't die.
My body does die,
but I don't die.
'cause I am the river,
the river of consciousness
that simply flows back,
into the ocean of consciousness.

What's This "Fight For Life"

In the name of saving life,
You continue to fight.

You fight for your image.
You fight for your body.
You fight for your concepts,
beliefs, and your pride.

How can you fight for life?
'Cause life is never threatened
nor does it ever die.

Not Ready

You say
"I am not ready
to be on my own,
to settle down,
to get married,
to have children
or to die"

My friend, look around in nature,
everyone lives on its own
when it's time to be on its own,
everyone tries to reproduce
when it's time for it to reproduce,
everyone also dies
when it's time for it to die.

Soul Knows No Concepts

Soul knows no
race, color or religion.
Soul knows no
name, culture or nationality.
Soul knows no
ego, duties or morality.
'Cause
At birth, your soul is shining through,
but, it doesn't know the language,
hence, it doesn't know the concepts.

Birth And Death

I will die again because I was born again.
Thanks to my awakening,
I am not coming back again.

I play in this world like an innocent child.
Now, I will never get lost
In the past and the future.

I met the wicked whore of the silver and gold.
Now, I will not be lured
by the shiny, glittery gold.

I live in the clear world of real God.
Now, I will not be afraid
of the ghosts of my thoughts.

The universe exists because of real Me
Now, I will never lose touch
with the real God in Me.

One day, I will leave the stage of this world.
I will leave this form
to assimilate in the *formless*.

Dr. Zaidi's Quotes

- Keep your mind where your body is.

- Your conditioned, busy mind is the root cause of your stress. You are not born with this. You acquire it from your society as you grow up.

- The past and future are mental abstractions, virtual and unreal. The present moment is the only *real* thing. Live in it if you want to live a *real* life.

- Many people live a conditional life. In their minds, certain conditions have to be met before they will start living their life. That day never arrives, because they keep adding more and more conditions and goals.

- Excessive thinking about the future is the major reason for fear, anxiety and panic attacks.

- You can only solve a problem if it exists, but your busy mind creates a virtual problem, and then, it tries to take care of this phantom. How absurd!

- Frustrations arise from expectations, which originate from your conditioned mind.

- Most human interactions are actually based upon "conditioned minds interacting." That's why there is so much stress in our lives.

- You can be free of your conditioned mind simply by observing it in action. Don't hate it or you will make it stronger. Simply observing it is enough.

- Conditioned mind can never know what unconditional love is.

- Live in your field of awareness, created by your five senses: what you see, hear, taste, smell and touch. If it is not in your field of awareness, it is unreal for you at that moment.

- Keep asking yourself two questions: "Is it happening right now, at this very moment, in my field of awareness?" and "What is happening right now in my field of awareness?"

- True living is like watching a movie, playing continuously around you and realizing that you are also in the movie.

- Concepts divide human beings, and that is the basis of conflict and violence. True freedom from violence lies in freedom from concepts.

- Concept is not reality and reality is not conceptual.

- We all live in a conceptual world and mistakenly take it for real.

- Any descriptive God is a conceptual God, far from the Real God.

- Real GOD is all around you and inside you. It cannot be described because language itself is conceptual.

- Science is the religion of the modern world.

- The source of stress as well as joy lies inside you.

- Make the ultimate choice to be stress-free without any outside help.

- Logic is the ultimate asset we humans have.

- Get rid of the filters created by your conditioned mind. Then, take a fresh look at your life with the lightning rod of *logic.*

- You don't die only if you are not born.

- Hell and Heaven are emotional states, not walled communities.

- Free yourself from the Virtual Self in order to be stress-free in this life and the life after death.

About Dr. Zaidi

Dr. Sarfraz Zaidi, MD is a leading Endocrinologist in the USA. He is a medical expert on Thyroid, Diabetes, Vitamin D and Stress Management. He is the director of the Jamila Diabetes and Endocrine Medical Center in Thousand Oaks, California. He is a former assistant Clinical Professor of Medicine at UCLA.

Books and Articles:

Dr. Zaidi is the author of these books: **"Power of Vitamin D", Reverse Your Type 2 Diabetes Scientifically" , Wake Up While You Can" , "Stress Cure Now", "Hypothyroidism And Hashimoto's Thyroiditis", "Take Charge of Your Diabetes," Graves' Disease And Hyperthyroidism, and "Stress Management For Teenagers, Parents And Teachers."** In addition, he has authored numerous articles in prestigious medical journals.

Honors:

In 1997, Dr. Zaidi was inducted as a Fellow to the American College of Physicians (FACP). In 1999, he was honored to be a Fellow of the American College of Endocrinology (FACE).

Speaker/Teacher:

Dr. Zaidi gives lectures to the public as well as the physicians. He has been interviewed on TV, newspapers and national magazines. He taught resident physicians at the Endocrine Clinic at the Olive-View UCLA Medical Center, a teaching hospital of UCLA.

Internet:

Dr. Zaidi also writes extensively on websites including:

www.OnlineMedinfo.com which provides in-depth knowledge about endocrine disorders such as Thyroid, Vitamin D, Parathyroid, Osteoporosis, Obesity, PreDiabetes, Metabolic Syndrome, Menopause, Low Testosterone, Adrenal, Pituitary and more.

www.DiabetesSpecialist.com which is dedicated to providing extensive knowledge to Diabetics.

www.InnerPeaceAndLove.com which is an inspirational website exploring the Mind-Body connection.

He has done educational **YouTube videos** about Vitamin D, Insulin resistance, Diabetes, Prediabetes, Heart disease, Thyroid diseases, and Stress Management.

You can access these YouTube videos as well as extensive health information from his main website:
www.DoctorZaidi.com

Other Books by Dr. Zaidi

Wake Up While You Can

Using the torch of logic, Dr. Zaidi leaps us into what life after death is. His insight is original, logical and a breath of fresh air, free of old religious ideas and concepts.

Dr. Zaidi's logical approach to spirituality is a true milestone discovery. Dr. Zaidi uses logic to elaborate:

What is your likely fate after death.

How you can easily change this fate during this life-time, simply with wisdom provided in the book. Then, you are stress-free in this life and in life after death.

You are extremely lucky to be a human being. Only as a human being, can you change what your life after death will be. Only as a human being, can you bring the sorrow cycle of rebirths to an end.

Therefore, <u>wake up while you can</u>, as a human being.

Stress Cure Now

In his ground breaking book, Dr. Zaidi describes a truly NEW approach to deal with stress. Dr. Zaidi's strategy to cure stress is based on his personal awakening, in-depth medical knowledge and vast clinical experience. It is simple, direct, original and therefore, profound. He uses logic - the common sense that every human is born with.

Using the torch of logic, Dr. Zaidi shows you that the true root cause of stress actually resides inside you, not out there. Therefore, the solution must also reside inside you.

In **"Stress Cure Now,"** Dr. Zaidi guides you to see the true root cause of your stress, in its deepest layers. Only then you can get rid of it from its roots, once and for all.

Stress Management For Teenagers, Parents And Teachers

Using the blazing torch of logic, Dr. Zaidi cuts through the stress triangle of teenagers, parents and teachers.

This original, profound and breakthrough approach is completely different from the usual, customary approaches to manage stress, which simply work as a band-aid, while the volcano underneath continues to smolder. Sooner or later, it erupts through the paper thin layers of these superficial strategies.

Dr. Zaidi guides you step by step on how you can be free of various forms of stress. From peer pressure, to stress from education, to conflict between teenagers, parents and teachers, to anxiety, addictions and ADD, Dr. Zaidi covers every aspect of stress teenagers, parents and teachers experience in their day to day life. Dr. Zaidi's new approach ushers in a new era in psychology, yet this book is such an easy read. It's like talking to a close friend for practical, useful yet honest advice that works.

Reverse Your Type 2 Diabetes Scientifically

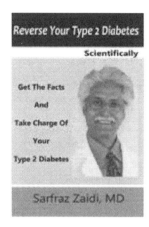

There is a common misconception among patients as well as physicians that treating Type 2 diabetes means controlling your blood sugar by any means. This approach is dangerously flawed. The fact is that Type 2 diabetes is a complex disease process. If not managed properly, it often leads to a number of horrendous complications. Sometimes, medications can cause more harm than good.

In "Reverse Your Type 2 Diabetes Scientifically," Dr. Sarfraz Zaidi, MD explains what is the root cause of Type 2 diabetes. Then he showcases his unique 5-step approach to manage this disease at its roots. Over the last fifteen years, he has employed this groundbreaking approach to help thousands of Type 2 diabetic patients. He has included actual case studies from his clinical practice to illustrate how his 5-step approach can reverse Type 2 diabetes as well as its complications. Dr. Zaidi's unique 5-step approach consists of:

1. A simple, yet profound approach to Stress Management, based on his personal awakening.

2. A revolutionary, scientific approach to diet. You may be surprised to learn how Calorie-based dietary recommendations are actually *not* very scientific. His diet is based on actual food items you buy in your grocery store or farmers market. He has included 75 of his own recipes. He also gives you a practical guide to eat at home or eat-out at various ethnic restaurants.

3. A new, scientific approach to exercise. You may be surprised to learn how too much exercise can actually be quite harmful.

4. An in-depth, scientific description of vitamins, minerals and herbs that are valuable in managing Type 2 diabetes.
5. Prescription medications, when necessary. A comprehensive description about: How various medications work, what are the advantages, disadvantages and side-effects of each drug.

Hypothyroidism And Hashimoto's Thyroiditis

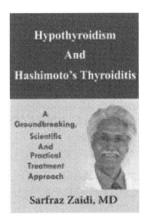

The current treatment of Hypothyroidism is superficial and unsatisfactory. Patients continue to suffer from symptoms of Hypothyroidism, despite taking thyroid pills. Even worse, there is no treatment for Hashimoto's Thyroiditis, the root cause of hypothyroidism in a large number of patients.

Dr. Sarfraz Zaidi, MD, has made a breakthrough discovery about the real cause of Hashimoto's Thyroiditis, and how to effectively treat it. He has also made new insights into the causes of Hypothyroidism. Based on these ground-breaking discoveries, he has developed a revolutionary approach to treat Hypothyroidism and cure Hashimoto's Thyroiditis.

In "Hypothyroidism And Hashimoto's Thyroiditis, A Breakthrough Approach to Effective Treatment," you will learn:

- Why do you continue to suffer from symptoms of Hypothyroidism, despite taking thyroid pills?
- What really is Hypothyroidism?
- What are the symptoms of Hypothyroidism?
- Why is the diagnosis of Hypothyroidism often missed?
- Why is the current treatment approach to hypothyroidism unscientific?
- Why are the usual tests for thyroid function inaccurate and misleading?
- What actually causes Hypothyroidism?
- What is the root cause of Hashimoto's Thyroiditis, besides genetics?
- What other conditions are commonly associated with Hashimoto's Thyroiditis?
- How do you effectively treat Hypothyroidism?
- How do you cure Hashimoto's Thyroiditis?
- And a detailed thyroid diet that works.

Graves' Disease And Hyperthyroidism

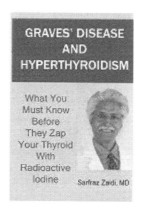

Graves' disease is one of several causes of hyperthyroidism. In "Graves' Disease And Hyperthyroidism," Dr. Zaidi, describes how to accurately diagnose and treat Graves' disease as well as other causes of hyperthyroidism.

The medical treatment of Graves' disease has not changed in over 50 years. Sad, but true! The standard, usual treatment with Radioactive iodine is a superficial, myopic approach. It almost always makes you hypothyroid (underactive thyroid state). Then, you need to be on thyroid pills for the rest of your life. In addition, radioactive iodine does not treat the underlying root cause of Graves' disease - autoimmune dysfunction, which continues to smolder and easily erupts into another autoimmune disease. Anti-thyroid drugs do not treat autoimmune dysfunction either. They provide only temporary relief. Often, symptoms return once you stop these drugs. Surgery also does not treat autoimmune dysfunction. It often leads to hypothyroidism as well as many other complications.

Over the last ten years, Dr. Zaidi developed a truly breakthrough approach to get rid of Graves' disease at its roots - autoimmune dysfunction. His patients have benefited tremendously from this approach. Now, its time for you to learn about this ground breaking discovery.
Dr. Zaidi reveals what really causes autoimmune dysfunction that ultimately leads to Graves' disease. His revolutionary treatment strategy consists of five components: His unique Diet for Graves' disease (including original recipes), the link between Vitamin D deficiency and Graves' disease, the connection between Graves' disease and Vitamin B12 deficiency, how Stress causes Graves' disease (and Dr. Zaidi's unique strategy to manage stress) and the Judicious use of Anti-Thyroid drugs.

All books available at Amazon.com and
other online retailers.

Life P.59

Made in the USA
Lexington, KY
28 July 2016